HowExpert Presents

How To Teach The Bible To Children

Your Step By Step Guide To Teaching The Bible To Children

HowExpert with Anne Snyder

For more tips related to this topic, visit HowExpert.com/teachbible.

Recommended Resources

- HowExpert.com – Quick 'How To' Guides on All Topics from A to Z by Everyday Experts.
- HowExpert.com/free – Free HowExpert Email Newsletter.
- HowExpert.com/books – HowExpert Books
- HowExpert.com/courses – HowExpert Courses
- HowExpert.com/clothing – HowExpert Clothing
- HowExpert.com/membership – HowExpert Membership Site
- HowExpert.com/affiliates – HowExpert Affiliate Program
- HowExpert.com/writers – Write About Your #1 Passion/Knowledge/Expertise & Become a HowExpert Author.
- HowExpert.com/resources – Additional HowExpert Recommended Resources
- YouTube.com/HowExpert – Subscribe to HowExpert YouTube.
- Instagram.com/HowExpert – Follow HowExpert on Instagram.
- Facebook.com/HowExpert – Follow HowExpert on Facebook.

From the Publisher

Dear HowExpert reader,

HowExpert publishes quick 'how to' guides on all topics from A to Z by everyday experts.

At HowExpert, our mission is to discover, empower, and maximize talents of everyday people to ultimately make a positive impact in the world for all topics from A to Z...one everyday expert at a time!

All of our HowExpert guides are written by everyday people just like you and me who have a passion, knowledge, and expertise for a specific topic.

We take great pride in selecting everyday experts who have a passion, great writing skills, and knowledge about a topic that they love to be able to teach you about the topic you are also passionate about and eager to learn about.

We hope you get a lot of value from our HowExpert guides and it can make a positive impact in your life in some kind of way. All of our readers including you altogether help us continue living our mission of making a positive impact in the world for all spheres of influences from A to Z.

If you enjoyed one of our HowExpert guides, then please take a moment to send us your feedback from wherever you got this book.

Thank you and we wish you all the best in all aspects of life.

Sincerely,

BJ Min
Founder & Publisher of HowExpert
HowExpert.com

PS...If you are also interested in becoming a HowExpert author, then please visit our website at HowExpert.com/writers. Thank you & again, all the best!

Table of Contents

Introduction

So, you want to teach the Bible to children! This is a worthy goal and a great ambition! I hope this book will be a blessing to you as you start teaching children about the Bible, the best book of all! If you have already walked this path for years, maybe this book will contain some new ideas about how to be even more effective.

Keep some things in mind as you begin reading this book. First, I intend this book to be an encouragement to you. The goal of this book is to help you in practical ways and to provide you with tips you can put to work in your teaching ministry. It is a step-by-step book with practical steps and hints as to how to teach God's Word to the children you have the chance to teach!

The book is not only to increase head knowledge, but to help you in practical ways to learn to teach the Bible to children. You may not see all the results you are hoping for on the very first day, or on your very first try, but practice makes perfect, or at least it helps. What is practiced is ever properly learned. You must give it your best effort because you can do it with God's help. You too can become an "expert" at teaching God's Word. So, let's get started!

Chapter 1: Goals

You need to think about why you want to teach the Bible. It is helpful to have concrete goals for any project you undertake and especially when you teach the Bible.

What motivated you to want to teach the Bible to children? Perhaps you just volunteered (or were drafted!) to teach one of the children's Sunday School classes at church, and need some ideas. Perhaps you have always wanted to reach out to your neighbor children and are considering starting an after school club.

Don't just think about why you decided to teach the Bible to children. Think about what you want to accomplish by teaching the Bible to children. Is your purpose teaching them all the stories of the Bible or helping them to know God, the author of the Bible? Is your purpose to correct help them develop good habits that will help them in their lives?

I believe that one of the best goals we can have in teaching children, is the goal that their lives will be changed, to know and follow God. This does not happen overnight. It takes time,energy and repetition,. It also takes living out an example of how the Christian life ought to be lived.

Chapter 2: Qualifications

It is important to remember that not just anyone can be an effective teacher when it comes to the Bible. However, don't worry. You can be a good Bible teacher, but first you must be prepared.

- The first step when teaching the Bible to children, is to know the Bible . You cannot teach efficiently what you do not know.
    - Like any good teacher, you need to know your subject matter!
    - Imagine, for example, someone who knows absolutely nothing about math trying to teach math to a group of children. The teacher doesn't even understand the basic principles, but just reads out of a book to the children . A child raises his hand to ask for help: "Teacher, I tried to do the problem just like you said, but it didn't work. What did I do wrong?" The teacher does not know, because the teacher never understood the subject in the beginning. Some bright children may catch on from what the teacher read, but the average child will not learn much from a teacher who does not understand the subject .
- One must also love the Bible, for one can only teach superficially what one does not love.
    - Let's just say there were two teachers trying to teach Spanish to a class of children. The first loves Spanish, her best friends are Spanish-speaking, she

loves to go out in the evenings and talk in Spanish to her Spanish neighbor children. The second grew up in a family where Spanish speakers were always criticized as too lazy to learn the country's language, and constantly annoyed by the children in school who said rude things about her behind her back in Spanish. She now teaches Spanish, not because she loves it, but because it's a job that pays.

Which one will be able to impart most successfully to her students the art of speaking this foreign language? Obviously, the one who loves the subject! Her students will catch her excitement. They will catch the vision and long to one day speak Spanish as well as their teacher.

- Besides loving and understanding the Bible, you must also understand the children that you teach..
  - Have they learned from the Bible their whole lives or have they never even heard basic stories?
  - What is their home situation ? What do they face or have to deal with at school? What kind of truths will be the most helpful to them?
  - Learn their vocabulary. What words do they use to express their thoughts?

For example, if you are trying to communicate the word "proud", they might express with other phrases such as "stuck up" or perhaps with even more newfangled phrases that were not yet in use when you were their age.

- Explain words,to make sure the concepts you are trying to get across are truly expressed. Some groups of children may like deep thoughts and know advanced vocabulary. Others may be learning English as a second language and need very basic vocabulary.
  - Others may just not have been as exposed to Bible language. In this case, simplify.
  - A great teacher is not the one who has the most sophisticated lesson, but the one who gets the truths across the best! What kinds of things are the most important to them? What interests them?
    Taking these things into account can increase the effectiveness of communication in teaching.
    I believe children can feel love and interest. If you really care about them and are interested in their lives, they will sense this. Often they will not be interested in what we have to tell them until we are interested in what they have to tell us, in what matters to them.
- Lastly, but not of least importance, you must not only know the Bible, love the Bible, and know and love the children. You must also know and love the One who wrote the Bible, the One who knows and loves the children more than any human could ever love them. Namely, you must know and love God before

you will be able to effectively communicate His Word.

It is paramount not just to know well the particular lesson that you are about to teach, but to have a true and living relationship with God.

- Spend time in His Word and in prayer daily. If you do not have a true relationship with God, you may teach the children many things and you may impart facts from the Scriptures, but it is doubtful that you will impart anything more than that. It is doubtful that you will be able to lead the children into a true relationship with God. It is also doubtful that you will be able to teach them truths that will radically change their lives if you do not have a changed life yourself: a life of loving, serving, and following God.

Chapter 3: Methods

There are certain broad methods when it comes to teaching the Bible. We most often think about teaching the Bible through a Bible lesson. Teaching a good Bible lesson is an art , and there are many ways to go about it.

However this is not the only way to teach children about God's Word.

- Teach the Bible through songs. You can communicate a lot of truths through songs. Songs are often retained when lesson content and details have been long since forgotten. Think of songs you learned as a child that you still remember today!
- Another way of teaching the Bible is through direct memorization of Scripture verses. In this way the children learn succinct truths from God's word. There are many ways to teach the verses, which will be discussed below.
- Another way to teach the Bible is through skits or puppet shows. Some children learn best when they act things out. Take advantage of this. Sometimes for a change of pace, you can get the children to do an impromptu skit based on the lesson you just taught.

Let's examine each in detail, and see the benefits each method brings into the overall process of teaching the Bible to children.

The Bible Lesson

First, there is the lesson. The lesson, for younger children, will often consist of a story in the Bible. Children like stories, and therefore stories are a very good way to keep their attention, and at the same time to teach the Bible's truths..

God,in the Bible, has revealed to us where we come from, how bad things occurred , how He gave us His Word, the history of His people and how we can have salvation in Christ. The individual stories in the Bible are part of this big picture. Yes, there are parts of the Bible that are not stories. These parts are important too, but often truths contained in those parts can be emphasized through the stories. For example, consider the story in Exodus 16 about how God sent bread to His people in the wilderness with a miracle of manna from heaven. There is more to this story than an getting bread from heaven. You can enforce truths taught in other passages such as:

- God sees everything and hears all that we say.
- We should not complain, but be thankful to God.
- We should pray and talk to God about any problem we have, like Moses did when the people complained.
- Whatever God says is true. He said the manna would go bad if they kept it overnight, and it did. We should always listen to God, because He knows best.

These truths, taught in other places in the Bible (the Psalms, the epistles) are also taught through this story, and can be easily incorporated. Thus we see that the Bible lesson is very important. Children often remember a story line well and, when they remember the story line, they can remember the other truths that are connected to the story.

Songs

Music is a great way to teach the Bible to children. There are songs whose words are Bible verses set to music. Other songs recount stories in the Bible, such as "Peter and John Went to Pray." Still other songs communicate Bible truths in an attractive and memorable way. Finally, there are songs that teach about the Bible, such as singing the books of the Bible set to music so that the children will learn the order of the books .

Bible Memory

Memorizing Bible verses is also an important aspect of teaching the Bible to children.. The truths contained in the memorized verses can come back to the children years later when they need that truth in order to make correct decisions in life. AWANAS and Scripture Memory Fellowship both have good curriculum to help children to memorize verses.

However, if you are not using either of these two programs, don't neglect this important aspect of Bible memorization. You can teach the children one Bible verse each week along with your lesson.

There are many ways to teach the verse, and each has its own particular value.

- My grandmother would have the children read the verse with her ten times, and by the end of this exercise, they all knew it. Sometimes you can add variations to the reading. The first time read it softly, the second time loudly. The third time have those who ate cereal for breakfast read it, the fourth time those who didn't eat cereal, the fifth make the children say it standing on one foot, etc. Be creative!
- Some children learn best if you have them learn the verse with signs that go along with the words. If you know sign language, you can use the official signs, but if not, create your own, or even better, let the children help you.
   o Sometimes you will be able to put the verse to music.
   o You can write the verse on a white board, and erase one word after each time you read it, till they are saying it with nothing at all left to look at.
   o You can write out the first letter of each word as a memorization tool, after the children are familiar with the verse, but don't have it quite memorized
   o One key to verse memorization is review. Review the verses you have already learned. What is reviewed often sticks much longer in the mind. Don't just learn a verse once, and never go

over it again. Sometimes, if time permits, you might review not only the verse from last week, but also from previous weeks. Each week, review the verses from the last five or ten weeks. This will help reinforce the verses in the children's mind, so they will be a permanent addition to their mental repertoire, not just a one-time hit and run.

Drawing

Some children enjoy drawing. You can have them draw out the major events in the story. I did that as a child, and it helped me to think through the events. You can also have them draw word pictures that are used in the Bible, or other concepts. If you are doing a study on the Lord's prayer, for example, you can draw a throne for the phrase, "Thy kingdom come" and a loaf of bread for "Give us this day our daily bread."

Acting

Do a skit based on the Bible lesson. This could be something you practice for weeks and put on for the parents, or it could be an impromptu rendering at the end of the lesson to review. The account of Jesus' birth is often acted out for Christmas programs so many children know this story. However there are many other stories that are rarely acted out, and might make an interesting production sometime.

Biblical truths such as helping those in need, working hard, etc are good subjects for acting. You can act out the story of the Good Samaritan, or make up your own situation that illustrates how to respond to others who need help, how to be kind to your siblings, how to help your mom, and many more.

Once again, be creative. You do not need to be the world's best acting troupe. Use what you have. Costumes are optional. Find whatever props you can, and do without what cannot be easily come by, especially when you are doing an impromptu skit!

Scripture Reading

Finally, when it comes to methods of teaching the Bible to children, do not neglect having the children actually read the Bible.. Encourage this. It is one thing to feed a young child, but as he grows older, you have to teach him to eat. When I was seven-years-old, my mother set me to reading the book of James, and told me to draw pictures of all the word pictures I found there. I enjoyed this simple task, and remember to this day drawing pictures of the object lessons contained in this book such as that of the tongue not being able to be tamed, works being dead without faith, and thorn bushes not making figs, etc.!

Don't forget, methods are almost as endless as teachers! You must take into account the group you are working with as well as the setting.

Chapter 4: The Lesson

We already discussed some of the benefits of using the classical form of the lesson to teach the Bible to children. This tool is so effective, that it merits a chapter to itself to delve into some of the how-to regarding this special art of communicating the Bible in a way children will understand and remember.

First, when it comes to teaching Bible lessons, there is the question of content. What are you going to teach? Are you going to follow a book of lesson plans? What series of lessons do you want to use?

There are many different approaches. Let's look at the benefits of several different routes you could take.

- First, there is the chronological approach. This approach starts at the beginning with who God is, with creation, the fall, with all the key stories in Genesis and Exodus. The lesson plan then moves on to other major events in the life of the people of Israel, their entrance into the promised land, and the time under the judges, the kings, the prophets. After this is, the life of Christ , along with a salvation invitation. You can use the rest of the New Testament history from Acts and the epistles if you want. This approach is the most effective when you have a class that you will be able to teach for an extended time.
- There are others who believe that whatever the lesson or whatever the topic, a salvation invitation should always be made. The problem with this approach is that children often do not

know the basic truths necessary for a true conversion, and are in need of basic teaching before such an invitation even makes sense to them.

- Of course, Christ is the central point of the Bible, and some prefer to jump straight to the life of Christ when teaching children. Christ's life truly is important, and children can learn a lot from His example and teaching. It is not beyond them to understand the basic concepts of salvation, and how Christ died on the cross in their place for their sin, so that they can be saved and have peace with God.
- Some prefer to have lessons on a theme, such as how God cares about children. You can develop different series about the parables of Christ, or His miracles.
- My mother developed a curriculum for the quarter before Christmas. She summarized the whole history of the Old Testament by teaching about the most important promises of Christ's coming. (That He would be born of a Woman, Of the Seed of Abraham, a Son of David, etc.)
- You can do a study on prayers in the Bible, or on the Lord's Prayer in particular. You can study a particular book of the Bible.

The options when it comes to content for your Bible lessons are almost endless—with a range as broad as from Genesis to Revelations!

Lesson Preparation

Now you must start in earnest to prepare the lesson. This, of course, takes time, but the time spent on lesson preparation is worth it. The well-prepared lesson not only turns out better in the end, but is more effective in communicating the truth of God's word. A sloppy job when teaching the Bible is not acceptable.

- Keep in mind that you must know what you teach, and you must know it thoroughly. Read the passage or passages that you are teaching . Seek to know the content well that you hope to teach to the children. Ideally, lesson preparation starts several days before you have to teach the lesson. Don't try to cram it all into the last few hours.
- Read the passage several times, until the details stick into your head. Then you will be able to tell the story freely without having to seek to memorize every last word.
- When teaching a lesson, another important aspect is prayer. Commit the lesson to God in prayer. Ask Him what He wants the children to get out of the lesson.
- It is very important when teaching a Bible lesson to realize that you must depend on God. You, by yourself, may be able to craft an interesting story, but without God's help, no lasting good will come of it. Several times I have been completely out of ideas about how to teach a particular lesson, but once I realized that I can't do it in my own strength, I I prayed and ask for help, God gives me such great ideas that it turns out to be a very interesting lesson

that the children enjoy.

- Think. Thinking is a key to success in many parts of life, and preparing a good Bible lesson is definitely included.

- Think about how to make the lesson interesting to the children. Think about what key truths you can teach from this lesson, about what parts of the story you especially want to emphasize.
- Think about questions you can ask to keep the children involved as you go along. For instance, when I was preparing the lesson about how the Israelites traveled for three days in the wilderness without finding water, I made up a question that I could ask to get the children thinking. I asked them if it had ever happened that they had been out of water. Then I asked them if they liked it when that happened and went on to have them imagine what it would be like if they not only didn't have water, but couldn't borrow some from a neighbor, or couldn't buy some at any store to wash with, to drink, etc., for three days.
- Make a plan. Plan what you want to say. Some may be helped by writing an outline of the most important events, and other thoughts that you want to include. Others make a mental plan. Perhaps you have curriculum with a lesson outline ready-made. Whatever you do, make the lesson plan your own. Have it well ingrained in your head, so even if the children ask an unexpected question, they will not throw you off track and you will not lose your train of thought.

- Practice is an important part of lesson preparation, especially at the beginning of your career in teaching. Practice the lesson out loud and,if you are going to be using visuals of any sort such as pictures, flannel graph, or other objects, it is a good idea to practice with the illustrations.

Visuals

You can use visuals to enhance your lesson. Visuals come in many shapes and sizes.

- There are Bible picture sheets. These are often great visuals, especially when well-drawn with realistic figures, and they are easily handled.

o Sometimes Sunday school curriculum comes with pictures.
o At other times you will have to purchase your own. There are many different places that you can order or purchase these.
o You can even draw your own simple pictures of the story progression.. Some illustrations you think of that would add to your lesson might not be available for sale. For example, I was teaching a lesson about Jesus' birth to a group of 5-8-year-olds. As I was thinking about what I wanted these children to understand from this lesson, I realized three things:

- These children would see no connection between the chronological lessons they had so far up to Abraham, Jacob and Joseph, and the story I was now going to teach them about Christmas .

- The children would have no idea how much time had gone by between Abraham and Jesus' birth.
- These children, living in our society in which single moms are not out of the ordinary, would not have any real concept of what a miracle it was that Jesus was born of a virgin.

o So what could I do? I had an idea. I decided to take the genealogy in Matthew chapter 1 and draw a figure to represent each person from Abraham to Christ.

- I drew a simple figure and wrote the name listed in the genealogy beside each man whose name was listed, .
- Beside each man, I drew a woman, his wife, and wrote the woman's name when I knew it. I did this for all 40-plus men in the list. I drew yellow crowns on the heads of those who had been kings.
- Finally at the bottom, I drew Mary without a man.
- As I taught the lesson, I showed them how Jesus was connected to Abraham.

- I showed them how much time had passed, how many people had lived from the first event to the second.
- I showed them how Jesus came from the kingly line, and thus it made more sense to them when I explained how the angel said that Jesus

would sit on the throne of his father David.

- I told them that each man had a wife, and that no woman could have a baby without a man, and that it was a great miracle that Christ had been born with no human father.
- Flannel graphs are another option. This is great for kids, as they like seeing the figures, and it catches the attention of many children. This is slightly harder to use than picture sheets but you can easily master it

  o If your church has a flannel graph set available for use, take advantage of it.
  o If not, and if you are thinking of teaching the Bible to children long term, you might even consider investing in one yourself. You can easily purchase deluxe felt sets, either large or small, from a variety of internet sources.

- Sometimes the best visuals are objects. If, for example, you are teaching a lesson, from Isaiah 40 about who God is; you might consider taking along a bucket with a drop of water in it, a scale with a piece of dust on it, and a little dried grass, to illustrate the relative smallness of humankind in relation to the greatness and permanence of God.

Sometimes you can combine a number of the above ideas, and you use than one kind of visual in your lesson. It is a good idea to use some variation in presentation approaches from week to week.

Lesson Delivery

How you present the lesson is a major part of teaching the Bible to children. Perfecting this skill comes with practice, but there are certain tips that you can follow to help you on your way.

- Be excited about the lesson yourself. Present the lesson in a bold and confident way, with obvious excitement conveyed through your facial expression and eyes. Speak clearly, not too quickly and not too slowly.
- Be dramatic. Obviously, this does not mean to be hilarious or use comedy that will distract from the lesson, but move your arms and your body to help the children get into what is happening in the story.
- Be prepared. When using visuals, be prepared. Know how to arrange the flannel graph on the board and when to put on the newest pieces.
- Look at the children. Eye contact is one way of engaging the children.
- Ask questions. Keep the children involved. Children will listen better when you keep them engaged.

Chapter 5: Reviewing the Lesson

Lesson review can be done in a variety of ways. There are several primary ways, and then one can always make variations based on these models.

- Retell. Ask the children to retell the story. Often you will need to prompt the children by asking a few questions. Let one tell a few sentences, then allow the next to speak.
- Question/Answer. This is probably the most often used way of reviewing the lesson, with review questions to ascertain the children's level of understanding and/or attentiveness.
- Visual/kinesthetic review.

Now that we have identified the basic categories, we will explore each in more depth.

- Retell. Retell can be done in various ways.

- First and most elementary is the simple retell, where the children simply retell the story. However there are more interesting ways to carry out a retell review. If you have a number of children, stand them in a circle with a ball. You start the retell with the first sentence of the story, then throw the ball to anyone you want . The person who catches the ball has to continue the story for a few sentences, then he or she must throw the ball to someone else. This continues until the story is completely told.

- If you used picture sheets for telling the lesson, you can give each sheet to a different child and have them go and stand in line and get in order based on the pictures, so the pictures will be in the order in which the events happened.
- If you used flannel graph for the lesson, and if you have a lot of time, have a few children retell the story using the flannel graph, or give each child a piece, and have him put it on when you get to that part in a short recap of the story.

- The second broad type of review game is a question and answer oriented review. For this you will need to prepare questions (if none are provided), ask questions over the facts of the lesson, the central truths of the lesson, and anything else that you want to review or that you want to see if they have learned.

- Once again, there are many variations. You can split the children up into two teams, and award a certain number of points for each correct answer.
- You can put the children at a start line, and allow one step forward for each correct answer.
- You can have a simple picture or design and cut it into as many pieces as you have questions. Each child who answers a question receives a piece, and then at the end (or as you go) they have to put the picture together like a puzzle.
- You can have a disk toss, using old CD's, and let each child who answers correctly have a shot to see if he can throw the disk into a box.
- The ideas are almost endless. There are many

prepared review games that come with the lesson material, but other ideas can be found on the Internet or made at home. You can even invent your own review game.

Chapter 6: Application

Application is very important when teaching the Bible to children. untilt? Thus, in our lesson, we must draw conclusions about how to live out the truths learned. These conclusions should not be abstract, but simple things that apply to the lives of the children.

These practical conclusions can be things contained expressly in the lesson. For example, in the lesson about Daniel and the lion's den, we can emphasize that the children must serve God no matter who makes fun of them. Teach them the importance of prayer to God. Teach them that we need to trust in God, because God has the power to protect us. You can share specific situations when we need to trust God. For example, when we are scared of a thunder storm, when someone we love is in the hospital, etc.

When the lesson is about the Israelites in the wilderness who continually forgot how God was taking care of them and had worked in the past to provide their needs, teach the children to remember what God has already done for them. Encourage them to make a list of things that God has done for them in the past, and when they are discouraged, to get it out and remember God's goodness, and that He is trustworthy. Don't forget to teach that complaining is wrong, and that it displeases God, who hears everything that we say.

You can ask them the following week how they put into practice truths that they learned in the previous lessons, to see if these truths are impacting their lives.

Remember that the goal of your teaching is not that the children have more head knowledge. Yes, this is important too, and can be a great help in their lives, but the most important thing is that the truth they are hearing remains with them and actually changes their lives in how they talk, how the act, and how they think. The goal is for the children to know God and to be pleasing to Him, not just that they know the Bible facts and can win a Bible quiz, or answer all the questions right after the lesson.

How To Lead a Child to Christ

When we talk about application, it is important to remember several facts. First, the ultimate goal for teaching the Bible to children is that the child will come to a true relationship with God. Some children may come from Christian homes where they have been taught from God's word and what it means to follow Him all their lives, and may already have entered into this relationship. For other children, the Bible and its teachings may be altogether new, and it may take time for the child to learn them and to decide whether or not to accept them and make them his own. Some children have grown up in Christian homes all their lives, yet they still have never have turned to Christ for salvation and hope. Some of them might even have the mistaken idea that because they grew up in a Christian home and know all about following Christ, that makes them Christians.

It is important that you understand the basics of salvation, and can point a child to Christ while explaining how he can have a true relationship with God and what it means to follow Him.

- First of all, it is important to keep in mind that you never want to force a child into a profession of salvation. This can be very detrimental to his spiritual life, as he may think that he is saved when he is not. Later children can struggle with doubt and turmoil for years wondering if they were really saved, if they were too young or did not really understand what they were doing when they made a profession of salvation.
- You, as the teacher, must realize what salvation is, and what it is not.

- A true conversion is not just praying a prayer. Do not force children to pray a prayer to be saved, just because you wish they would get saved, or just so you can tell others about the "results" of your teaching.
- A true conversion is not just raising a hand. This may show interest, but make it clear to the children that you are just asking who is interested in learning more.
- A true conversion is based on God's saving work. It is based on true repentance over sins and true faith in Christ and His perfect life, His death in our stead, and His resurrection from the dead. True faith includes a complete surrender of one's life to God.
- A true conversion is not just a one day event when a child makes some sort of decision so as not to end up in hell if he dies. It the start of a life of obedience to Christ: a life of following

Him.

o To lead a child to Christ, you need to help the child to understand what conversion really is. You need to make sure that he understands the basic truths, and if he does not, you need to be able to explain them to him. Remember, even if he came to be counseled, this does not mean you should force him to make a salvation decision! He might not be ready yet!

- Make sure the child truly understands what sin is. Sin is not just a problem in and of itself. Sin is disobedience to God. Make sure the child not only understands what sin is, but also that he understands that he is a sinner and deserves God's forgiveness.. Emphasize God's holiness, and also His love and readiness to forgive. (Romans 3:23, Romans 6:23, Romans 3:10, etc.)
- Make sure the child truly understands what salvation is. Make sure he knows the basics about God, who Christ is, and what He came to do. Make sure He realizes that Christ died for us, and that He rose again, and is alive now in heaven. (John 1:12, John 3:16, 1 Corinthians 15:3-4, etc.)
- Make sure the child truly understands that conversion is a commitment to follow Christ, to belong to Him, to obey and serve Him. However do not confuse the child and lead him to think that we can earn salvation by being good. Stress that we cannot ever earn salvation by our works, because we can never be good enough. We have broken God's perfect law, and

only Christ can save us. Why? Because only He perfectly fulfilled God's law, and then died to be punished in our place, since we had broken God's law and disobeyed Him.

- If a child truly understands the truths about Christ's death in his stead, about who Christ is, and who God is. If he understands what salvation is, what it means to be a Christian, then you can lead him to conversion. (See Romans 10, John 3:36, John 5:24, etc.)
- Exactly what outward steps you urge the child to take depend somewhat on the culture. Obviously, true conversion is in the heart, a work of God, and a step of repentance, belief, and commitment on the part of the child. However you may want to encourage the child to pray, if this seems more appropriate, or to go forward in church. Be sure to encourage him to tell others what step he has taken.
- Share with the child what following Christ means. Share practical ways he can obey God. Encourage him to read God's word and to pray, to be involved in church, and to continue coming to Bible class to learn more about God.

Chapter 7: Get to Work

Children must learn more than just head knowledge, they must put into practice what they learned, and the teacher is no different. Until now, you have read many things about teaching the Bible to children. Now it is time to put them into practice!

Let's go step by step through what we've learned about preparing a Bible lesson, and see how you do!

- First, read the passage (in this case, Exodus 17—If you primarily use the King James Version, I would recommend reading it in other translations as well, because many children are not familiar with the vocabulary used in the King James Version, and will greatly benefit if you use modern words when you teach them):
- Okay, you read the passage (I hope!). Did you read it only once, or did you read it several times? Do you feel that you have a good grasp of the chapter's contents? If you didn't understand all the words, read it in other translations, or look up the words in a dictionary or Bible dictionary. What you don't understand yourself is very hard to effectively pass on to others, and if you didn't understand the words, chances are that children will understand them even less.
- Read the passage several more times until you feel that you know the details almost as well as if you had experienced it yourself.
- Don't forget to pray and ask God for wisdom in preparing this lesson, depending on Him to

give you wisdom.

- Now, think. Think about the lesson. Make a list of the main events. It is possible to make this list in your head, but it is often even more helpful to write it down. For example:

  o People continue their travels.
  o People don't have water to drink.
  o People complain.
  o Moses cries out to God.
  o God tells Moses what to do.
  o Moses does what God says (hits the rock with his staff), and God works the miracle.
  o Another people group (Amalek) attacks Israel.
  o Moses makes a plan to fight back.
  o Joshua and some fighting men fight against Amalek.
  o Moses goes up on the hill.
  o When his hands are up (evidently in prayer), Israel is stronger.
  o When his hands are down, Amalek is stronger.
  o Aaron and Hur help Moses keep his hands up.
  o Israel defeats Amalek with God's help.

- Okay, now you've listed the main events of the story. You will want to include these when you teach the lesson, but that is not all. You need to think of the truths that this lesson illustrates. Make a list of all the truths and applications of the story.

  o The people forgot how God had just turned bitter water into drinkable water and given them bread from heaven (chapters 15-16). They started to complain.

o   God heard them when they complained.
o   Moses heard them when they complained.
o   Complaining displeases God and shows we don't remember His goodness and we don't trust Him to take care of us now.
o   God knows when we complain too. He hears all we say and sees all we do.
o   Moses knew the right thing to do. Moses prayed to God in this troubling situation.
o   God gave Moses an answer and told him what to do to fix the problem.
o   God is the one who can help us when we have problems.
o   We too should turn to God in prayer when hard things happen to us.
o   We cannot fix our problems by ourselves, but God can.
o   Amalek attacked Israel, and Moses did something. He sent Joshua and the fighting men of Israel to fight against the enemy.
o   But Moses knew they couldn't win alone. He also prayed for the people, and the people won the battle only with God's help.
o   Aaron and Hur helped Moses when he was tired.
o   We should help each other, joining together to pray for others and to serve God together.
o   When we have problems, there is often something we have to do about it,like Moses sent Joshua and the men to fight,)but we also need to depend on God, because victory comes from God.

o   Once you have written these truths and

applications, think how you can combine all these truths and applications into the flow of the story .

o Sometimes you must draw from other passages to get further insight into the meaning of the passage you are teaching. For example, the New Testament comments on and explains many things in the Old Testament, such as the law that God gave on Mount Sinai.

o Next, decide what visuals you want to use. What visuals do you have available to illustrate to the children what happens in this story? Do you have picture sheets? Do you want to use flannel graph? Chose whichever method you think would work best, or whichever you have available.

o Practice the lesson. Practice it aloud. Don't be afraid to get off the computer and actually try it now!

o This lesson is best taught with actions, such as raising your hands when you talk about Moses raising his hands, and pretending you have a rod in your hand to hit the stone when you talk about that part of the story. Don't be shy. Children like actions. It might seem a little odd at first, but children are pretty open and accepting, and you should be willing to do what it takes to communicate God's truth most effectively to them. The more you practice, the more natural it will become.

o Now, think of review questions that you can ask the children. You can look back over your list from the passage and your list of applications and truths, and draw your questions out of these lists.

Chapter 8: Teaching the Bible to Your Own Children

There are different approaches to teaching the Bible. When you teach Sunday School, or when you teach a Bible club lesson, your approach will often vary from how you teach and what topics you use when you teach your own children. Your own children you have with you not just once a week, but every day for all the formative years of their lives. You can start when they are young, and keep at it until they are teenagers.

You will want to keep several factors in mind. First, there is the age factor. Not all children are at the same level. When your children are very young, teach them simple truths. You can use such helpful tools as Bible picture books or devotional books designed for small children.

Teach them simple verses that are only one phrase or one sentence long. Children can learn verses at a very young age, at two or three years old. As soon as they learn to talk, you can begin teaching them Bible verses by memory.

Be sure to sing a lot of songs. There are many songs teaching Bible truths in simple attractive ways. Young children will be able to learn and remember these songs, and will often even ask you to sing them with them. Be sure to use actions, as children love to move and will sometimes remember actions better than words, and the actions can help reinforce the words in their minds.

Elementary-age children are also a joy to teach. These children will enjoy Bible stories. When you teach your own children, you can approach these stories in many different ways. You can teach them in just the same way as you would teach other children in a Sunday school setting. However, you often will want to give your own children something more. Maybe they are attentive and good at listening. If so, you can read through the whole Bible with them, or at least all the story parts of it. Ask questions. Let them ask questions to see if they are understanding or not. Be sure to explain. This should not just be a boring activity. Make it interesting. Read to them, or let them read along.

Elementary-age children can learn longer passages by memory. Memorizing is good for children, and it helps them in other areas of their educational lives as well. You could try learning Psalms or other passages from the Gospels or the Epistles.

For example, once when I was a child, my family learned Psalm 148 together. To make this more memorable and easier to remember, we worked together on a project to make a poster illustrating each phrase in the verse. Here are instructions if you want to imitate this project:

- Verse 1: Draw a picture of heaven, for example clouds of glory or the throne of God.
- Verse 2: Depict angels in heaven bowing in worship to God.
- Verse 3: Let the children draw the sun and moon and stars to remember that even these heavenly bodies are also commanded to praise

God.

- Verse 4: Draw a picture of the water in the sky, perhaps in the form of clouds or rain.
- Verse 5: This verse speaks of how God created all these things. Think of a way that you can illustrate that fact in such a way as to clue yourself in about the verse when you see the poster.
- Verse 6: Perhaps draw a tablet (like the ten commandments were written on) to illustrate the fact that God made a decree regarding all these things, He established them, and what He says is final.
- Verse 7: For this verse, use your imagination to draw the ocean and the fish and other creatures that live in it. Even these animals are to give praise to God.
- Verse 8: This poster gives you lots of things to chose from, or you can seek to draw them all. Put on a snowflake, the wind, storms with lightening bolts. Or hail falling to the earth.
- Verse 9: This verse is quite straightforward to illustrate. Sketch on some hills, some mountains. Put on trees with fruit and evergreen trees.
- Verse 10: Here you will want to draw animals of all kinds, wild animals, domestic animals, and even birds.
- Verse 11: This verse is about people. Draw important people. Draw ordinary people. Be sure to draw crowns on the heads of the kings to help you tell them apart from all the other people.
- Verse 12: Here draw some younger people, maybe teenagers, both guys and girls. Draw a

grandfather and grandmother with some children beside them. Remember that no matter what your age or gender, you are to praise God through your life and your words.

- Verse 13: This verse is about praising God's name, about His glory. You can either try to depict God's glory, or simply write the name "LORD" in beautiful handwriting to remember that His name is exalted and we are to praise His name.

- Verse 14: This verse might seem a little more complicated to draw, but don't worry. You can either study what the verse is referring to by the word "horn", and seek to illustrate that, or simply draw more people praising God.

Let your children help you with each poster. Perhaps split the posters up between your children, and let each draw a certain number of posters. Assign the simplest ones to the ones who are not yet as creative or skilled in their drawing abilities. Perhaps none of you are very skilled artists. This does not really matter. Remember that this is not about beautiful pictures so much as an activity to help you and your children think about what this psalm is actually saying and what it is teaching us. These pictures can also be used as memory aids when you are reciting the psalm together. If you recite the psalm for others, the posters can help them think about the words you are reciting.

Other psalms that are nice to memorize (and can also be illustrated) are Psalm 1 and Psalm 23. Remember, you are not limited to well-known psalms. All the Psalms are inspired by the Holy Spirit, and you can choose any one of them to memorize with your children. Or if you rather, you can choose passages from the New Testament. Perhaps you want to learn parts of John 10 which talk about how Jesus is the Good Shepherd. Perhaps you want to learn a passage from James 3 about the tongues. These passages can also be illustrated, and teach important truths as well.

As children grow and mature, make sure you do not stay at the elementary level, teaching only Bible stories. Teach more in-depth. Teach what the stories mean, how they fit together. Teach about the prophecies of Christ's coming, the prophecies of His suffering, death, and resurrection. Perhaps you yourself have never really understood how all the Old Testament fits together. This is no excuse not to teach it to your children. Learn yourself, and then you can teach them. Teaching others is often a very valuable tool to help you learn something yourself.

If you feel like you are not well-versed in the prophecies regarding Christ's coming, here are some to consider and help you to whet your appetite.

- God promised (even while in the act of uttering the curses and punishment for the first sin) that Eve's Seed would crush the serpent's head, and that the serpent would crush His heel. This was the first promise that the Savior would come. Even when sin had entered the world , bringing despair and death, God promised a Savior, a Savior who would conquer the devil and would be victorious. The serpent crushing His heel refers to Christ's sufferings that He would go through to save us. However, in the end, He could not be held by death, but would rise from the grave and strike a death-blow to the devil. Not only did God promise to send a Savior, but He revealed how the Savior would come. He would not be an angel or a super-hero, but a human, someone who was born of a woman just like us.

- God promised Abraham that He would bless the entire world through his Seed. (Genesis 12:1-3) We read in Galatians 3:6-14 that in Christ all the nations in our world are blessed. This is the ultimate fulfillment of God's promise to Abraham that He would bless the world through Him.

- David also received a promise that the Christ would be one of his descendants. (See 2 Samuel 7) God promised him that he would have a descendant reigning on his throne forever. When the angel came to Mary (see Luke 1), he mentioned this promise of God, and that it was being fulfilled in her Son. We still do not see Christ reigning as king on an earthly throne, but He is the King of kings, and He will reign forever.

- Isaiah 7:14 is a well-known promise of God, proclaiming that the Savior that God would send would not only be King, but also that He would have a miraculous birth, being born without the help of any human father. This was fulfilled, as is recorded in Luke chapters one and two, and in Matthew chapter one.

- Micah 5:2 is another often-cited promise of Christ's birth, in which the place of Christ's birth was revealed by God hundreds of years before the event. God arranged everything so that Mary and Joseph traveled to Bethlehem in time for Christ to be born there, in the city of David just like the prophet Micah had written so many years ago. The Jews realized that this was a prophecy of the coming of the Messiah, and they even sent the wise men to Bethlehem based on this verse (see the story of the wise men in Matthew 2) when they came to Jerusalem asking about the One who would be born as the Jew's King.

- Numbers 24:17 records a promise of a star at Christ's coming.

This is by no means an exhaustive list. There are very many prophecies about Christ's coming. Once you have learned together about how God promised hundreds and even thousands of years beforehand that He would send a Savior to rescue humankind from their state of being enemies of God, then you can learn about how God also promised exactly what Christ would do for us.

- There is Isaiah 53, the well known chapter which speaks of Christ's sufferings, how he would be mocked, be beaten, and be meek when accused, be killed, bear our sins. It talks about what kind of grave He would be buried in, and even refers to the resurrection.
- There is also Psalms 22, referring to the crucifixion and describing the suffering of Christ, and how He would be forsaken by God.
- There is Zechariah 9:9 in which Christ's triumphal entry to Jerusalem riding on a donkey is predicted.

This list could go on and on . Research, learn , and pass the information on to your children .There is a curriculum called *Advent Foretold* which has some excellent lessons about how Christ's coming is predicted, complete with coloring pages and lesson helps with interesting information that portrays the miracle of such prophecies. Once again, one key to passing information on to your children is to be excited about it yourself. Show them that this is important to you by the expression on your face and the tone of your voice. Get them involved. Get them excited.

Besides teaching your children about prophecies, you should make sure they understand the Old Testament in general, and the many types that are found there of the work of Christ.

Teach them about the Levitical sacrifices, how the perfect lambs represented Christ, who died as the lamb of God to take away our sins. Teach them about the Passover, how the angel passed over the houses that had blood on the doors, and how Christ is our Passover, when we trust in Him and apply His blood to our hearts, God sees our faith and passes over us, so we do not fall under His judgment like those around us.

A good curriculum for teaching children about the Bible chronologically, and helping them to see how all the Old Testament prophecies fit together is the New Tribe's Mission's *Creation to Christ* set of lessons. These 50 chronological lessons present who God is and His plan to provide redemption for humankind.

Besides teaching the Bible chronologically or teaching about fulfilled prophecy, you can also do studies on prayer. Prayer is important for children, and is a way that they can move beyond knowing what the Bible says to knowing the One who wrote the Bible.

When my mother taught us about prayer, one of the subjects was the Lord's prayer. We often made little booklets on whatever topic we were studying from the Bible, and this was one of them. We made a little booklet about the Lord's prayer. We illustrated one page for each phrase of the verse. In this way we stopped to think more thoroughly about what we were learning, and not only did we contemplate what we were learning, we drew it andreinforced the teachings in our mind.

If you are interested in developing your own lessons over the key events in the Old and New Testaments, here is a suggestion for which lessons and Scripture passages to use:

- Teach about who God is. To truly understand God's word, it is important for children to at least have a basic working knowledge of who God is.
    - Teach them that God is the creator. This is covered in Genesis 1, but do not get into detail now.
    - Teach them that God is forever, that God is great and Powerful. Isaiah 40 has many wonderful comparisons that you can use.
    - Teach them that God is the author of the Bible, that He had His prophets write

down His Word. Now it is compiled into
our Bible.

- o Teach them that God knows everything.
  (See Psalms 139)
- o Teach them about God's love and
  justice.
- o This list is by no means inclusive. Teach
  them what you know about God, what
  you think is the most basic for them to
  grasp. It is true, many children will
  already know the basics, but for those
  who do not, it is important to be sure to
  touch on them.
- o You do not have to go into depth on each
  of the above points. They will be brought
  out into more clarity in future lessons
  through the truths learned about how
  God worked with His people.

- 1. Teach about creation. (Genesis 1-2) Teach
  how God created the whole world, and how
  everything was perfect at the beginning.
- Teach about the fall. Genesis 2:16-17, Genesis
  3. Teach about God's command, and how man
  disobeyed, and the consequences.
- Teach about Cain and Abel. (Genesis 4) Show
  that man must come to God in faith.
- Teach about the flood, man's disobedience,
  God's judgment, and how God rescued Noah
  who lived for Him and believed Him. (Genesis
  6-9)
- Teach about the Tower of Babel, and how God
  once again judged man's disobedience. Explain
  where different languages and nations came
  from. (Genesis 11)
- Teach about Abraham's obedience to God, and

how God promised to bless the world through him. Stress how God counted him good and righteous by his faith. (Genesis 12, 15)

- Teach about Abraham's faith and how God blessed him with the son. He had promised even when it seemed impossible for Abraham to have a son since he was so old (Genesis 19-21).
- Teach how Abraham offered Isaac to God in faith. (Genesis 22) Make an analogy to how God gave His only Son, who willingly gave Himself as the sacrifice for our sin.
- Teach about Jacob and Esau. (Genesis 25-33)
- Teach about Joseph, and how God worked evil together for good. (Genesis 34-50)
- Teach about the children of Israel, and how God worked for their good through Moses' birth. (Exodus 1-2)
- Teach about Moses, as the leader of the children of Israel, and how God chose him. (Exodus 4-5)
- Teach about how God used the plagues to deliver His people. (Exodus 5-15)
- Teach about how God provided for His people in the wilderness (Exodus 16-17)
- Teach about how God gave the law and the Ten Commandments (Exodus 19-20)
- Teach about the Israelites' rebellion and idolatry. (Exodus 32)
- Teach about how God established the tabernacle and the sacrificial system as a way of atonement. (Exodus 40, Leviticus)
- Teach about how God brought His people into the Promised Land. (Joshua 1-6)
- Teach about how the Israelites lived under the

judges. (Excerpts from the book of Judges)

- Teach about the kings of Israel.
- Teach about how God promised to build David a house, with one of his heirs on the throne forever. (2 Samuel 7)
- Teach about how God's people continually fell into idolatry and disobedience, and were warned by the prophets.
- Teach about how the people were exiled to Babylon.
- Teach about how God brought a remnant back to the land.
- Teach about the announcement of Christ's coming, and His birth.
- Teach about Christ's obedient life, His baptism, His temptation, and how He never sinned.
- Teach about how the Lord Jesus went around doing good, teaching, and healing. Use several concrete examples of how He healed, and how He taught. You might want to include such passages as John 3 when Jesus stressed the need for the new birth; John 4, and how Jesus said He was the water of Life; John 6, where He showed how He was the true bread that descends from heaven; and John 10, where he taught how He is the Good Shepherd.
- Teach about Christ's betrayal, His sufferings, and His death. Teach why He diedfor our sins. Make a reference to the Passover lamb,John 18-19
- Teach about Christ's resurrection! Without Christ's resurrection, all else is without purpose. Luke 24
- Teach about Christ's post-resurrection appearances, and his ascension to heaven. Acts

1

- Teach about Christ's sending the Holy Spirit, and the beginning of the Church. Acts 2

Chapter 9: Teaching the Bible Throughout the Day

We tend to have the view, which is partially correct, and partially mistaken, that Bible teaching is a specific lesson held at a specific time with specific children. This is correct in the sense that we should set apart such times. We should devote specific time to teach the Bible to our own children, and to the children in our Sunday School classes or Vacation Bible Schools. It is important that we emphasize the Bible, and give it priority, with specific times set aside specifically for learning from God's Word.

However it is a mistake if you think that these Bible lesson times are the only times that you should teach children about the Bible. The Bible is relevant to all of our lives. Part of the purpose of teaching the Bible is to see lives transformed, and life transformation comes from putting truth into action. You can suggest and describe truths that need to be put into action during the Bible lesson, but when you have the time to actually live with children, you can help them to begin living out God's truth in their personal lives in many even more practical ways.

How can you do this? Teaching God's Word to children throughout the day also has several aspects.

- First of all, you can and must live out God's Word in your own life if you want those you are teaching to put it into practice. It is unrealistic to imagine that your children or the children you are teaching will become better at obeying

God's word than you are.

- If you teach them to honor your parents, but at the same time they hear you complaining to others about having to help your aging parents, your teaching will seem disqualified in their minds.
- If you have a lesson about the ten lepers, only one of whom came back to thank the Lord Jesus, this is a wonderful lesson. You might stress at the end that we too should be thankful, thanking God and others for the good things that we receive. If, however, you are always complaining about the bad weather, the hot classroom (after all, why haven't they done something to get the air conditioning into your classroom too?!), or the child who misbehaves, they are more likely to learn from your actions and attitudes than from your words, learning to complain rather than to be thankful.
- On the other hand, if you always live out what you teach, they will learn from your example. They can learn from your example even if you have never specifically taught that lesson. For example, if they see you come each Sunday, and drop off the old grandmotherly lady who can barely walk by the front door, personally helping her to her seat, they will learn to care for those with needs, to respect those who are older, even if you have never had a lesson on this subject.
- If your children see you reading God's word and spending time praying, they will value these habits, even if you have not taught a series of lessons on what prayer is, or on how God wants us to read His Word.

- Secondly, we teach children about the Bible throughout the day by commenting about the things around us.
- In the first place, these comments can be about nature, God's amazing handiwork.

  o Maybe you are outside and see a beautiful sunset. You can comment to your children about how God is the One who made the sky and who gave us this beautiful sunset.
  o If you see a rainbow, you can tell them that this is God's promise that He will never flood the earth completely again.
  o Maybe you have a bird feeder. As you watch the different kinds of birds come to the eat the seeds, you can teach your children that God designed each bird, that He is the Creator. You can tell them that each bird lays eggs that hatch into more baby birds of the same kind, because that is how God created them, to reproduce after their species.
  o If it happens that you are outside sometime and see a bird that fell out of a nest, or even one that died, you can tell them that God knows each bird that falls to the ground, and if God takes care of these insignificant birds, God will take care of us even more even if we sometimes feel insignificant.
  o Maybe you have pet animals or fish. You can teach your children that God created all animals. You can show them the various features of His design--the way the fish's gills allow it to absorb oxygen out of the water, the way a cat's eyes narrow into slits

when it is bright, or reflect light when it is dark.

o Perhaps you are out driving at night somewhere where it is dark enough to see the starry sky. Tell your children that God created the stars and that He is great, greater than the whole universe. Tell them that He knows the name of each star—He is that wise and all-knowing.

o When you look outside at the clouds, you can point out the beauty that God created.

o When your children are afraid of storms, tell them that God sends out the lightning, and that even the lightening and the thunder have to obey Him, and that He is more powerful than any storm. Tell them that God gives rain to water the plants. Tell them how Jesus calmed a storm when the waves were so big that the disciples were afraid they would drown.

o Maybe you have some house plants, or like to go outside. You can show them the beautiful flowers that God made, and how each one is different and lovely. If God makes the flowers so beautiful and "clothes" them. He can give us clothes to wear and help us with the things we need.

o Point out the beauty of trees, their leaves, their fall colors. Show them how trees bear nuts or fruit because that is how God made them.

o If you are out in the garden, you can teach them how each plant makes seeds and that God made the plants not only to be beautiful, but also to give us fruits and vegetables to eat.

- Tell them that weeds came as part of the fall, and when we are hot and sweaty outside because we have to work hard and pull weeds, that is *not* how God made things in the beginning, but rather a result of sin.
- You can even draw analogies, such as that if we only pull off the top of a plant, and don't get out the root, the weed can grow back, and the same is true for sins in our lives.
- Teach them how God made us too.
- Even when they are sick you can teach them how sickness is a result of sin and the fall, but how God loves us and made our bodies so that they know how to fight disease so we can get better after being sick.
- If you go to a wedding, you can remind your children how God created marriage, and His plan from the beginning is that a man and woman be faithful to each other all their lives.
- When someone you know has a new baby, remind your children that each person is created by God, and that God loves each one.

- Teach children about God not only from nature, but also in various situations that come up.

  - Perhaps your child is playing with another child, and the other child hits him. You must teach your children how to respond in love to those who do unkind things to them.
  - You can teach your children to share

with each other, to share toys, to share special treats they receive. In this way you can teach your children in the practical situations of life how we are to treat others, what the Bible teaches us.

o Sometimes unpleasant things will happen. Maybe your tire goes flat when you are going grocery shopping with your children. Stay calm. Teach your children that God will help you. Teach them that sometimes God allows hard things to happen to help us so we learn to trust Him more, to know that He will take care of us. Tell them that even bad things God can work out for good when we love Him.

o Maybe someone has died. You can teach your child what the Bible teaches about resurrection, and that if we trust and follow Christ, we can be with Him after we die, and that the body dies, but this is not the end of life.

o Thankfulness is something that it is important to teach to children. Encourage your children to be polite, to say please and thank you. Tell them that God is the one who gives us all good things, and that we need to say thank you to God as well.

• Teach your children to apply specific Bible truths.

1. Some truths are specifically taught in the Bible and can be learned better by example than by a

Bible lesson. For example, teach your children to pray. Pray with them. Model how to thank God for your food before you eat, but do not stop there, with quick prayers before meals. Teach children to pray when they have problems. Teach them by doing it with them. When you have that flat tire, pray and ask God for His help. Then thank Him afterward for how He helped you.

2. Teach your children to be kind to others. Teach them to greet others, to respect their elders, to help out at home.

3. Teach your children to work. The Bible teaches us that we are to work hard and not be lazy. Teach your children to do simple tasks around the house. This teaching is more than just telling them. It is lovingly training then, punishing them when need be, so they will learn to be the kind of children (and later adults) that God wants them to be.

4. Teach your children to give. This can help them learn not to be selfish. When it is Christmas time, teach them that Christmas is not only about getting. We should give to others. You could prepare shoe boxes for poor children in another country. You could help each child to make simple gifts for each of his siblings, or his cousins, his grandparents, or even his friends. If you are out of ideas for helping your children make gifts, here are some simple suggestions:

   o Paint an ornament. You can often buy wooden ornaments that can be painted and given as gifts. These are simple projects completed quickly.

   o Make a sock doll.

o Make special treats (peanut clusters, cookies, etc.). You will probably have to help your children, but let them actively participate so they learn to joyfully give to others.

o There are many other ideas as well, if you cannot think of anything yourself, search the internet or find a book with ideas.

- Sometimes you will have opportunities you would rather not have when you must teach children from God's Word when someone you know has done something that is not according to what the Bible teaches.

o Perhaps someone has committed some types of sin. Teach the children that God's Word teaches us that such actions are wrong. (For example, stealing, lying etc.)

o These kinds of situations are not pleasant. We would rather they had never come up, but since they did, we must teach children even through these situations about what is right and what is wrong according to the Bible.

Chapter 10: Teaching the Bible to Children Learning English as a Second Language

Teaching the Bible is sometimes more difficult than at other times. Depending on the part of the country you live in and on your particular church or Bible club setting, it is possible that you will have children who speak some other language more fluently than they do English. In such situations, you will either have to teach them in their language (if you have someone who can speak it), or you will have to teach them using English.

We will consider the first option briefly, then move on to the second, as it is probably the more likely of the two to happen.

First of all, you have the option of teaching these children in their native tongue. In the area of the United States of America where I live, the prevalent minority (in some neighborhoods actually a majority) is Mexican. Some Mexican children understand better in Spanish than in English. This is especially true for children who have not yet spent extensive time in the schools where they quickly learn English, and also children who have recently moved to America. My sister and I would teach these children in Spanish, as we were learning it ourselves in school as well as by talking to our neighbor ladies in Spanish.

For teaching in a language that is not your first language, there are several things to keep in mind.

- It is important to read the passage over several times. Sometimes if it is short, you might even want to memorize the passage that you will be teaching from.
- Try to use a modern translation of the Bible, so the words you use will be familiar to the children. If you have a bilingual friend who knows the language better than you do, ask him or her about words that you think the children might not know, and what would be better substitutes for those words.
- Sometimes memory can be used as a substitute for fluency. If you are not yet fluent in the language, carefully write out a lesson, seeking to use the correct verb tenses. If possible, have someone who knows the language well correct this first draft. Then, if necessary, memorize the lesson. (Of course this is not ideal, but sometimes it is necessary.)
- Use visuals. This is especially important. Visuals can convey a lot of information, saving you from having to explain things with words.
- Let them tell the story back to you. Listen to the way they express the concepts you communicated to them. Make a mental list of the words they use, and use them yourselves next time you teach. In this way you can learn the right way to phrase certain ideas, and the way they express certain concepts. Sometimes local dialects of a language vary from region to region, so the word the children use for a particular concept might not always be the word that you found when you looked the English word up in the dictionary.

o Other times, you will be teaching in English, but although you are fluent in it, the children you are teaching may only be learning it. In this case, care must also be taken to present the lesson in a way they will understand.

1. Talk slowly. Do not rush, as children are trying to understand and pick out words that they have learned.
2. Use visuals. If a child does not yet understand certain words, it could well be that he will be able to get the idea you are trying to teach through pictures. The pictures can help fill in the gaps in his understanding.
3. Be dramatic. Use your hands and face to describe actions and attitudes of the people in the stories.
4. Use simple words. Try to choose the simplest words. Often you can express the same idea in a multitude of ways. Try to pick the simplest way to express what you are teaching, using the best-known words.
5. Explain words. When you have to use words that are more complicated, be sure to take the time to explain. Explain complicated terms using simpler ones.
6. Involve the children. Have them repeat words after you at times. You might chose to have them repeat names of the key characters or of places. You might have them repeat a word that comes up often, after you explain what it means.
7. Ask questions. Do not force them to

answer if they do not yet feel confident in talking English. Sometimes children understand more than they can say. However if they do say the right answer, you can be confident that the message is getting across.

8. Use objects. Objects can help illustrate things, just as pictures or flannel graph.

9. Let the children help explain the story. If one child understands it better than others, let him explain it in his native language to the ones who know less English.

Let's go through the steps together for preparing a Bible lesson for those who are just learning English to try to put into practice the things we are learning. We already talked about how to prepare a lesson to teach. Some of the steps are the same, but you must take them each a notch further:

The first step is still reading the passage. If you do not read the passage, or know it by heart, where do you expect to get the ideas from to teach the lesson? Go ahead and read Exodus chapter seventeen again, this time thinking specifically about how to simplify it enough that children learning English as a second language will be able to understand the story line and the main truths.

- Read the passage, and read it again. Seek to read it several times, perhaps in several translations. Seek to use the translations with simple and modern words that children who don't know English well will understand. If you know any of the first language of the children you are teaching, you may consider reading the text at least once in their language too, so you can throw in a word from their language if necessary to help them understand.

- Read the passage until you know the details well, so well you can paraphrase it in your own words. Don't try to repeat the passage verbatim as it was in the Bible or the lesson book. Use simpler words on the level of their knowledge of the English language.

- Don't forget to pray. We always need to pray and depend on God, but in times like these, we can especially see His help, as He gives us ideas for simple words or ways to make the lesson more vivid and easier to understand.

- Now, think. Think about the lesson. Make a list of the main events. After you have made the list, go back and try to simplify each thing you have written. Sometimes you might think of other words that might not be simpler, but it could be that they are more common or easier to understand. Jot them all down in parentheses alongside your original outline. For example:

1. The people continue their travels. (The people keep going on their trip. They keep on walking, on and on. They are going where God told them to go.)

2. People don't have water to drink. (There is no water. There is nothing to drink. Oh no! What will they do?)

3. People complain. (This means the people talked bad about God, the people were not

happy. They did not say thank you to God. Instead they said bad things about God and that He was not taking care of them.)

4. Moses cries out to God. (Moses prayed to God. Moses talked to God about his problem. Moses told God that the people were not happy.)

5. God tells Moses what to do. (God told Moses how to fix the problem.)

6. Moses does what God says—hits the rock with his staff—and God works the miracle. (Moses did what God said. He obeyed God. He listened to God. What had God said to do? God said to hit the rock. Moses hit the rock. He did what God said. God did an amazing thing. God made water come out of a rock to give them water to drink.)

7. Another people group (Amalek) attacks Israel. (God's people had some enemies. Their enemies wanted to kill them. They wanted to fight against them and have a war to destroy God's people.)

8. Moses makes a plan to fight back. (Moses thought about what to do. He had a plan.)

9. Joshua and some fighting men fight against Amalek. (Moses' helper was named Joshua. He helped Moses when Moses needed help. Now he took some men and went to fight the enemies.)

10. Moses goes up on the hill. (Moses climbed the hill. A hill is like a little mountain. He walked up to the top of the hill.)

11. When his hands are up, evidently in prayer, Israel is stronger. (When Moses lifted up his hands and prayed to God, when he reached his hands up toward the sky, towards God, God helped. When Moses had his hands up towards

the sky, God's people were stronger. They fought better, they were winning.)

12. When his hands are down, Amalek is stronger. (When Moses got tired and put his hands down by his side, God's people were weaker. They didn't fight well. They were losing.)

13. Aaron and Hur help Moses keep his hands up. (Aaron and Hur stood by Moses and held up his hands.)

14. Israel defeats Amalek with God's help. (God helped his people to win the war. They won over their enemies.)

15. Okay, now you've listed the main events of the story, you've simplified them or written down other ideas of how to express the same concept with different words.

16. If it seems the lesson is getting too long or complicated, you might want to leave out certain details. For example you could leave out how Aaron and Hur helped Moses.

17. Now you will want to do the same thing to your list of main truths contained in the lesson.

○ The people forgot how God had just turned bitter water into drinkable water and given them bread from heaven (chapters 15-16). They started to complain. (The people forgot God's goodness. The people forgot how God always took care of them. The people forgot the bread that God gave them from heaven every morning. They started to say bad things about God. They started to think that God wasn't taking care of them.)

○ God heard them when they complained. (God heard everything they said. God knew they weren't happy with Him. God knew they wanted water.)

- Moses heard them when they complained.
  (Moses heard them too. He was scared the
  people would kill him.)
- Complaining displeases God and shows we
  don't remember His goodness and we don't
  trust Him to take care of us now. (When we
  talk bad about God or the things He has given
  us, God is not happy with us. God wants us to
  tell Him thank you for what He gives us. God
  wants us to remember that He is taking care of
  us and that He is with us.)
- God knows when we complain too. He hears all
  we say and sees all we do. (God knows
  everything we do and say. God sees all we do.
  He hears every word you say, even the bad
  words or the mean words.)
- Moses knew the right thing to do. Moses
  prayed to God in this troubling situation.
  (Moses knew what He should do. He did the
  right thing. He prayed and talked to God about
  the problem with the people. He told God what
  the people wanted.)
- God gave Moses an answer and told him what
  to do to fix the problem. (God told Moses how
  to make the people happy.)
- God is the one who can help us when we have
  problems. (God hears us when we talk to Him,
  and helps us with our problems.)
- We too should turn to God in prayer when hard
  things happen to us. (We can pray and talk to
  God about all our problems.)
- We cannot fix our problems by ourselves, but
  God can. (God can help us when no one else
  can.)
- Amalek attacked Israel, and Moses did

something. He sent Joshua and the fighting men of Israel to fight against the enemy. (Moses made a plan and Joshua started to do his part to fight the enemy.)

o But Moses knew they couldn't win alone. He also prayed for the people, and the people won the battle only with God's help. (Moses knew God was the only one who could help. That is why He told God about their problem. They could never have won if God hadn't helped them.)

o Aaron and Hur helped Moses when he was tired. (The two men helped hold up Moses' hands.)

o We should help each other, joining together to pray for others and to serve God together. (Help others! Help your friends when they need help! Pray for others!)

o When we have problems, there is often something we have to do about it (like Moses sent Joshua and the men to fight) but we also need to depend on God, because victory comes from God. (When you have a problem, do your part to fix it, but remember that God is the only One who is more powerful than anything. He can always help you.)

1. You may want to choose only a very few of these applications to especially emphasize, because if you seek to include all of them, you might lose the children you are teaching.

2. Give specific examples. For example, if you say that God can help us with our problems, list some problems that children might have, and some ways God can help them. (For example, if a child feels no one is his friend, if he is

68

struggling in a particular class at school, if his mother is sick, etc.)

3. Next, decide what visuals you want to use. What visuals do you have available to illustrate to the children what happens in this story? Do you have picture sheets? Do you want to use flannel graph? Chose whichever method you think would work best, or whichever you have available. Remember that visuals are especially important when teaching children who are not yet fluent in English. You might even want to go the extra mile to make sure the visuals are vivid and will correctly communicate the lesson content.

4. Practice the lesson. Often it takes special practice for the teacher to slow down, to use simple words, and shorter sentences. Put effort into practicing the lesson.

5. Be especially sure to use actions when teaching children that do not yet completely understand the English language. Think about how you can act out all the actions, not just the most drastic ones. Act out walking from place to place as they continue their journey. You might want to have the children themselves hold up their hands for a while to feel for themselves how soon one's hands get tired when holding them up.

6. You could even consider taking a little break in the middle of the lesson to make sure they are getting it. Have the children jog in place as hard as they can when you hold your arms up. When you put your arms down, tell them to just barely move and act like they are weak.

7. Use objects. When talking about not having water. Hold a cup of water in your hand. Talk

about how we like to drink water. Pretend to wash your hands. Tell the children we like to use water. Then pour out the water in the cup. Say the people had no water. Visually portray their dismay at the lack of water. Take a rod along with you, if you can find one. Objects drive home concepts into children's minds in ways that other things will not.

8. Review the lesson with simple questions. Make the questions simple with simple words. Perhaps refer to the visuals you use to help the children understand the questions.

These truths may be self evident, but still, unless one takes the time to stop and think, they might not ever come to mind. It is a special joy to see how children learning English can grasp truths that they would never have understood if we hadn't taken special pains in our preparation.

Chapter 11: Important Non-teaching Aspects

When teaching children, it is important to do certain things that do not fall directly into the category of teaching, but nonetheless have a direct impact upon the effectiveness of teaching.

- Pray for the children. We have already discussed how you must pray about the lesson you are preparing and realize that alone you cannot teach an effective lesson. However another very important aspect is praying for the children. Pray for their needs. Pray for their parents, their family situations. If you know of some problem or special need in their lives, pray especially for that. Pray that the children will come. Pray they will listen.
- Get to know the children.

- To effectively communicate with the children, it is very helpful to know them personally. Have you ever tried sharing your heart with a perfect stranger? I doubt it. We feel a little wary to share too much with someone we don't know well. Likewise we will pay the most attention to the advice we get from the people we know and respect the most.
- Ask them how they are doing. Ask them how school is going. Ask what they did for the holidays, if they like the snow, the hot weather, etc. Ask them about their family, how their siblings are doing.
- Tell them about your life. Maybe tell them

stories about when you were in school, or tell them how you celebrated Christmas, Easter, etc.
o   Seek to be more than just a teacher with a group of children. Try to become the children's friend, someone they want to share with andsomeone they look forward to talking with.

•   Help the children learn to know each other and be friends.

o   Involve all the children in your conversations. Let them get to know each other better.
o   Encourage them to help each other with the verse, the craft, or whatever needs doing.

•   Pray with the children. Encourage the children to pray. Maybe some pray all the time at home, but others might pray only rarely or never, if their parents have never taught them. Some may not know what praying is or how to pray.

o   Tell the children about prayer. Tell them that it is talking to God.
o   Encourage short prayers to start with. Explain exactly what you are doing if you have children who have not prayed much before. Tell them, for example, that today we are each going to say thank you to God for one thing that He has given us.
o   Maybe one member of the class is sick. Pray together for that child.
o   Remember, praying together strengthens bonds.

- Share together. Think of activities that can encourage sharing. For example when I taught the lesson about the children of Israel, and how they forgot how God had given them bread from heaven and began to complain again, I reminded the children that we should not forget what God has done for us. When hard times come, we should remember what God has done in the past, and trust that He is with us and will help us. I asked each child to share something that God had done for him in the past, and they told me neat stories about how they had a problem, and someone had prayed for them, and the problem had been taken care of.

   o These sharing moments help you know the children better.
   o It helps them know each other better.
   o It helps build unity among you as you realize that you are sharing things God has done for you.
   o It helps reinforce the truths in the lesson and tie them to everyday life.

- Make the children know they are special to you.
- Consider giving each a small gift at his or her birthday.
- Consider mailing post cards to children who are absent, telling them you missed them.
- Build Relationships with the Parents. Learning to know the children is crucial, but if you can take it a step further to get to personally know the parents, it is often an especially rewarding relationship. If the parents are believers, you

can encourage them in teaching and raising their children. You can partner together to lead the child into a closer knowledge of God and His word. If the parents are not believers, building a relationship with them can sometimes lead them to see the importance of what their children are learning. They can also be drawn towards God themselves. Here are some ideas that can help you build relationships with the parents.

- Chat with them if they come to pick up or drop off their children. Depending on your situation, you might or might not have this opportunity, but if you do, be sure to take advantage of it. Ask about work, their children, etc. Be sure to encourage them about their children, and mention it when their child was well-behaved, knew the answers, etc. Telling them can help build the relationship between you.
- Create social events that the parents are invited to. This might include a Christmas party at Christmas where you invite in the parents to eat Christmas cookies at the end of the Sunday School or Bible Club time. You could even invite them to your house for the party if you don't have a good opportunity before or after your normal lesson time.
- Host programs where the children sing songs they have learned, recite verses or poems, or do a skit, and invite the parents, allowing them to see what their children are learning.
- Sometimes you might be able to develop relationships with the parents by calling them on the telephone to touch base with the child.
- Take the time to visit the child's home. Perhaps

this will be when you invite the children, passing out fliers giving the date and time of the Bible-teaching event. Perhaps it will work just to visit for any reason. Take some cookies or something small, and, if invited in, you can chat with the parents. This will also give you a chance to get a look into what the child's home environment is like, whether positive or negative.

- If a child ever is in the hospital, you can go and visit him.
- Consider inviting the children to your home, not only at Christmas, but for any type of event you can plan. When their parents drop them off or pick them up, chat with them.
- If the parents are interested in Bible things, but do not know much about them, at times you can even offer to start a Bible study with the parents.

These hints are not directly for teaching children, but they are definitely something that can strengthen the influence that your teaching will have on the lives of the children you teach.

Chapter 12: Dealing with Distractions and Behavior Problems

1. What do you do with the children who just don't seem to listen? What do you do when one child is distracting the others, or with other distractions in the room or the place where you are teaching?
2. There are different solutions to different problems. Consider the following steps you can take to deal with distractions:
3. Seek to eliminate distractions. If you are having the Bible lesson in your house, and you have a cuckoo clock with a cuckoo that pops out and sings at the top of the hour, causing all the children to lose focus, consider removing the clock during the time of the lesson. If the children are playing with some object, take the object until the lesson is over. Return the distraction after the class and send a note home to the parents asking them to keep such objects at home. However, be sensitive to those shy or younger children that might need a blanket or stuffed toy during the first days of class.
4. Seek to lessen the influence distractions have on the children. If you are outside and the children are distracted by the cars driving by or mosquitoes that are biting them, consider moving inside if this is a possibility. If not, turn the children so their backs are towards the cars, or try spraying the place with some insect repellant before you start the lesson.
5. When the distractions cannot be either

eliminated nor can you lessen their influence, keep teaching. Do not allow yourself to be distracted by them, but rather keep teaching your lesson with purpose and direction, making sure to make your lesson interesting. When you do this perhaps the children will forget about the distractions as well.

6. Pray about the distractions, even while you are teaching. Pray for wisdom in dealing with them, and for God's help and strength.

7. Dealing with Problems among the Children

8. The children themselves can sometimes be the biggest distraction in the lesson. This is often caused by one of the following causes:

9. Children ask inappropriate or unrelated questions, interrupting the flow of the lesson.

10. Children talk to each other during the lesson.

11. Children bother each other (hit, kick, tease, etc.) during the lesson.

12. These distractions can also be dealt with in constructive ways.

- If the children ask inappropriate or unrelated questions, you may want to limit the questions you let them ask. You might tell them to save their questions until the end of the lesson. If they do ask the questions, either answer them briefly and get back to the lesson, or else ignore them, depending on the situation.

- If children talk to each other during the lesson time, it can sometimes help to separate the two children who are talking. Remind them that during the lesson they do not talk unless they raise their hand.

- If children bother each other in other types of ways, remind them of the rules. If they still do not stop, they might also need to be separated. If you have another leader or helper available, consider having him sit by or between the children who are causing problems. At times you might consider standing up and singing a motion song if they seem too restless.

- One important thing to remember is that sometimes it is more distracting to try to deal with each and every last thing the children do, then it is to just let them keep on doing it and continue with your lesson. Sometimes they are really listening when it doesn't seem like it. You have to use some discernment to know which things to address, and which to let go by.

Dealing with Children who Misbehave

Besides distractions during lesson time, children might be outright defiant, or just mischievous. They might not do what you say. There are a whole range of things that children have done in the past while they were at Bible Club or Sunday school. I myself have experienced children who ran and hid in the hall, children who played the guitar that was sitting in the room, children who stood on the tables, children who would not do anything I said, etc. Once again, you must have the wisdom to know which things to ignore and which things must be dealt with.

First of all, it is important that you, as the teacher, maintain an attitude of authority. Take charge. Be confident and lead. Often children will respond to your attitude of authority. On the other hand if you walk into the classroom just sure that you can't control the children and that they certainly won't behave, and they sense that this is what you think, they almost certainly will not behave. They will often live up to, or live down to your expectations.

Secondly, you might consider having some clear and simple rules, such as no hitting, no talking while the teacher is talking, etc. The rules will depend on your expectations for the children, as well as the specific areas that the children have problems with. It is usually wise not to have too many rules, as the children will likely forget some of them. Emphasize the things that are the most important.

You may consider making a child sit in a time out chair after two warnings. You may consider the possibility that if they still do not behave after a certain number of times of being reproved, they will have to go talk to the Sunday school superintendent or the Bible club director.

Sometimes if the situation gets bad enough, you may have to discuss the problem with the parents. This is usually used as a last resort, as talking to the parents can have any range of results. Sometimes it results in a true change in behavior. Other times the parent may make the child apologize. Sometime the parent might withdraw his child, or even all his children, from club, either because he feels insulted, or because he doesn't want his child to cause you problems.

Of course there are some types of discipline that are not appropriate in our culture in public settings. You should not, for example, slap or spank a child, and touching or restraining is often questionable. Be careful what you do so that no one will have any reason to say anything bad about you or to accuse you of things that are not true.

Chapter 13: Crafts to Reinforce the Lesson

The truths in the lesson can linger on much longer when you make a craft which is tied to the subject of the lesson. Consider making a craft with the Bible memory verse written onto it. Try to think of crafts that are directly tied to the lesson. You do not have to make a craft every week, but crafts can be ways of getting God's word into the children's homes, especially if they are from unchurched families. In general it can remind the child, when they see it, of what they learned in Sunday school or Bible club.

For example, when you teach the lesson about Moses praying and God giving water, and how he prayed and God gave victory over the enemy, your craft could take many forms. You could take card stock and make two praying hands (made by each child tracing around his own hands) and glue them together, folding the cuff of one hand out to the right, the other to the left if you want it to stand up. Then write the Bible verse on them. This can remind the children of the importance of praying about our problems, and thanking God for what He does for us.

Another option would be to find some small smooth stones, and write "God can do anything" on the stones. This can remind the children that water doesn't usually come out of stones, but God can do anything, and He gave His people water out of a rock.

You can use foam sheets to make shapes or collages out of. You can make picture frames out of Popsicle sticks and put a photo of the children who come to your class each week inside. You can make bookmarks with stickers on them or with the Bible verse. You can make cards or small gifts for their mothers on Mothers' Day, and their fathers on Fathers' Day.

Chapter 14: Finding the Children

This book is about how to teach the Bible to children, and all along we have proceeded with the assumption that you have children to teach. However this is not always a given.

Sometimes you inherit someone else's Sunday School class, children and all. They are desperate for a teacher, and so you quickly try to learn the ropes to be the best Sunday school teacher possible. Other times someone else starts a neighborhood Bible club and invites you to help. Once again, the children are provided without you having to look for them or gather them. Perhaps your church hosts a Vacation Bible School and the children come flocking by the dozens, and finding children is not something you need to think about.

Other times, God will lay a desire on your heart to teach children about God's life-transforming word. You will want to impart to others the life-giving truth that can help them find joy and fulfillment in knowing God. You may have a great desire to do so, but still you feel at a complete loss to know how to begin. You may have the time and commitment to prepare the lessons, as well as the money and resources to do crafts and activities, but you won't have any children to do them with unless you somehow find the children.

In such cases, there are several paths to pursue.

If you are seeking to start a weekly Bible club, or a summer club every night for a week, in your own neighborhood, you can go out and invite the children personally. Perhaps you already know their parents, and can just give them a call to invite the children to come over at 10 a.m. on Saturday morning. Perhaps you want to invite children you don't know. Get a friend or family member to help you, and go from door to door, knocking and inviting children. Have a printed invitation to leave with them so they can remember the date and time, and can see a list what you are planning to do.

Sometimes if you want to see if there is interest, you can hold a special Christmas party, and invite those who attend to come back for weekly classes. Perhaps you want to try holding a summer five-day Bible club. Whichever you decide on, the invitation can help the children keep the times and dates in their head. It can also appeal to them if you list the different activities that you will be doing.

This is not the only way to invite children. You can invite children from your church, and tell each one bring an unchurched friend. You can have your own children invite their friends from school, baseball practice, etc.

If you are really ambitious, you can even start an after-school Bible club in any school that offers other after-school programs, and pass out the invitations in their classrooms. My family did this, and this is the tenth year that we have been able to have this ministry, touching the lives of many children and sometimes even their families.

In all this, remember that your personal example and testimony plays an important role. If you do not live a consistent Christian life, there will be parents who will not allow their children to come. On the other hand, we once had a neighbor man who said that the only reason why he let his daughter study the Bible with us is because he saw that we were different, not living like the people who claimed to be Christians but cheated their employees, or lived in other ways that should never characterize true Christians. This perceived (and often actual) hypocrisy often closes the door to being able to minister to others or their children.

Chapter 15: Combating Discouragement

Teaching the Bible to children is not always easy. Sometimes you will have a hard day. Maybe only two children came for the second week in a row. Maybe it seemed no one listened at all. Maybe two children fought and left angry at each other and at you, for trying to stop the fight.

- Hard days come. When you have such times, you must remember why you are doing this. You are not doing this in the first place for yourself, to make you feel good about life, or to make yourself feel fulfilled. These feelings will often follow, and there can be great joy in teaching when you see the children applying the truth you have been teaching them in their lives. However, even when things are hard, remember that you didn't get into teaching children because it would always be easy and fun.

- Remember that you are not even doing this first and foremost for the children. Yes, you are doing it for them. If it were not for them, you would not bother going into all this effort. You truly love them and care about them, and you want them to learn from God's word, and learn to be godly people. However this does not always happen overnight. Sometimes it does not happen at all. Even children can reject God's truth.

- First and foremost, you are, or should be, doing this for the Lord Himself. He is the One who has commanded us to go and tell all about Him, to train them to walk in His ways. He is the One who will ultimately reward us for faithful service. He is the One who sees not only the results that other people can see, that we like for others to notice;how the children we teach are learning truth, how they now behave better than they once did, etc. He sees all our preparation time, all our effort. He sees every motive of our heart, if we are really doing it for Him, or only for ourselves or the praise that comes from others.

- Remember that even if only a few children come, God may be preparing those few children to serve Him in large ways, and to someday reach out to many more than you could ever have reached alone. Commit the results into God's hands.
- Pray for guidance and help. Pray for the children. God can give wisdom so we know how to deal with difficult children. He can encourage us when we see that only a few come consistently.

Conclusions

We have discussed many things here! Just like you want the children to put into practice the things they learn, I hope you will be able to put the tips you have learned in this book into practice in your career of teaching the Bible to children. I hope that what you have read here will not remain information stored in your brain, but will become living practice, giving ideas that help in the practical aspects of teaching and communicating God's truth to children, resulting in changed lives.

Keep in mind that you will reap what you plant. It might take years and it might be hard work. But God can cause His Word to bear fruit. Sometimes children's work can have even greater results than you expect. For example, once we held an Easter Bible club for our neighborhood children. Some of the mothers who came to pick up their children were also interested in learning God's word. Through this contact with them, we were able to start a ladies' Bible study which changed the lives of at least one family, beginning with the mother, and spreading to the father, who changed from being an abusive alcoholic to taking his family consistently to church and inviting others. The children, in turn, have been helped to walk in God's way, as they are now attending church on a regular basis and learning from God's word.

Other times, results may not be seen. We had spent close to a year teaching a neighbor girl, when she lost interest. She is now a teenager, and still doesn't show much interest in the Bible, but God's word was sown in her life, and later, God can bring it to her mind and use it to draw her towards Himself through the lessons from the Bible she heard many years back.

Other times, children take God's word to heart. Perhaps they are from Christian families, but their parents do not take the time to regularly teach them from God's word. I have a friend who tells me how there was another lady who took time to do a weekly children's Bible club with her and three other children, and because of that, she is now motivated to teach others, and is my co-teacher. We are reach, working together with me to start a Sunday-school type class in a small church plant. Besides the class she is teaching with me in one village, she has also started a Sunday school in another village church, reaching out to many children. This is all because someone took the time when she was young to teach her about the Bible week after week, even when the attendance at the weekly class was only four children.

Remember, when you teach God's Word, you are not just teaching math or writing or some other school subject which can be useful to the children later in their lives and careers. You are teaching them the powerful and living Word of God which can help them both in their future lives here on earth, and helping them to find eternal life and a relationship with God . If you have teaching the Bible to children on your heart, don't put it off! Get started now!

About the Expert

Anne Snyder has been teaching the Bible to children for over ten years. This career of teaching began with her desire to reach out to the neighborhood children. She attended a training session with Child Evangelism Fellowship, but has gained most of her experience by teaching children. The Lord has enabled her to teach children in three countries and in three languages. Anne has been involved in an after-school Bible club, in village children's ministries, in day-camps, and in her church's Vacation Bible Schools. She considers it a great blessing to see how God uses His Word to work in their lives and the lives of their parents.

HowExpert publishes quick 'how to' guides on all topics from A to Z by everyday experts. Visit HowExpert.com to learn more.

Recommended Resources

- HowExpert.com – Quick 'How To' Guides on All Topics from A to Z by Everyday Experts.
- HowExpert.com/free – Free HowExpert Email Newsletter.
- HowExpert.com/books – HowExpert Books
- HowExpert.com/courses – HowExpert Courses
- HowExpert.com/clothing – HowExpert Clothing
- HowExpert.com/membership – HowExpert Membership Site
- HowExpert.com/affiliates – HowExpert Affiliate Program
- HowExpert.com/writers – Write About Your #1 Passion/Knowledge/Expertise & Become a HowExpert Author.
- HowExpert.com/resources – Additional HowExpert Recommended Resources
- YouTube.com/HowExpert – Subscribe to HowExpert YouTube.
- Instagram.com/HowExpert – Follow HowExpert on Instagram.
- Facebook.com/HowExpert – Follow HowExpert on Facebook.